LAND THAT JOB!

16 Simple Steps to Discover Your Career Passion

Becky Gosky

CONTENTS

Title Page	1
DESCRIPTION	5
INTRODUCTION	6
ABOUT THE AUTHOR	7
Chapter 1:	8
Step 1: Reflect on your childhood interests	10
Step 2: Identify what drains and energizes you	12
Step 3: Write out your ideal lifestyle	14
Step 4: Take reputable personality tests	16
Chapter 2:	18
Step 5: Survey your friends and family	19
Step 6: Ask coworkers and supervisors to describe you	21
Step 7: Define yourself	23
Step 8: Seek wisdom	24
Chapter 3:	27
Step 9: Sample new media	28
Step 10: Engage your senses	29
Step 11: Go somewhere new	30
Step 12: Try different industries	32
Chapter 4:	33
Step 13: Follow your intuition	34

Step 14: Make your case   35
Step 15: Say "no" to low priorities   36
Step 16: Cling to what motivates you   37
CONCLUSION   38
AUTHOR'S NOTE   40

DESCRIPTION

Are you fresh out of high school and ready to take your first steps into the wild world of adulthood? Maybe your 30th birthday is tomorrow and you are still stocking shelves at that dead-end job you took eight years ago to pay the bills. Perhaps you are nearing an early retirement at the firm, but you feel as though you have more to offer the world in a field you have yet to pinpoint.

Trying to figure out the magical combination of "what I'm passionate about" and "what I'm good at" can be daunting for most.

Never fear! *"Land That Job! 16 Simple Steps to Discover Your Career Passion,"* is exactly what you need to discover the career you have been dreaming of.

INTRODUCTION

Are you fresh out of high school and ready to take your first steps into the wild world of adulthood? Maybe your 30th birthday is tomorrow and you are still stocking shelves at that dead-end job you took eight years ago to pay the bills. Perhaps you are nearing an early retirement at the firm, but you feel as though you have more to offer the world in a field you have yet to pinpoint.

Trying to figure out the magical combination of "what I care about" and "what I'm good at" can be daunting for most. By reading, "*Land That Job! 16 Simple Steps to Discover Your Career Passion*," and following its steps, you can overcome that challenge and soon discover your career passion.

So, splurge on a good quality journal or notebook, grab a pen, and follow the steps below, recording your thoughts as you go. You deserve this time. When you invest in yourself, good things happen for you.

"The first step is to know where you are, acknowledge where you are, and be aware of it. Then, start taking action to get where you want to be." Danny Beriman, Your GPS for Life

ABOUT THE AUTHOR

Becky Gosky lives in the mountains of North Carolina with her husband, two sons, Mom, and two dogs. After spending many years working in human resources and real estate, she now enjoys sharing her expertise as a freelance writer and author. In addition, as a certified coach, she also helps others follow their hearts and passions so they can lead more fulfilled lives whether in a job or their own business. It's a journey she understands on a personal level.

CHAPTER 1:

Discover Yourself

"You've got to know yourself so you can at least be yourself." –D.H. Lawrence

What would you say if a potential employer asked you to list your strengths and weaknesses? Or, in an interview they asked you the expected question, "tell me about yourself." These types of requests are meant to discern the kind of person you are. The potential employer not only wants to define your skillset, but they wish to discern if you are the kind of person they would enjoy having around the office. Are you a good teammate? Are you conscientious? Do you speak confidently in meetings, sharing information of value? Do you volunteer to help when there are deficiencies in the schedule? Are you an interested, compassionate friend? Do you encourage positive office morale? Are you honest and trustworthy?

However, if you are not sure of all of these things and more for yourself, how can you possibly explain it to someone else? The following first four steps will help you better define just that.

A story to provide perspective:

From Aesop's, "The Donkey and the Wolf."

Message: Always be True to Yourself.

The Story: There once was a donkey munching sweet new grass in a pasture. Near the pasture was a wood where a wolf was lurking, ready to pounce.

The donkey spotted the predator and, thinking quickly, devised a plan to save himself. He started pretending he was injured and in quite a lot of pain.

The wolf came up to the donkey in curiosity and anticipation of dinner. "What caused your injury?" he asked of the donkey.

"Oh, please pull it out!" Moaned the donkey, feigning severe pain. "If you do not pull this large thorn out of my hoof, it might cut you as you swallow me down…ouch!"

The wolf certainly did not want the thorn to cut his throat as his meal went down, so he bent down to carefully and closely examine the donkey's hoof.

Just then, the donkey kicked out with the might from his powerful legs. The wolf yelped in pain and tumbled several yards away, dazed.

While the wolf gingerly got back up to strike, the donkey had already galloped away to safety.

"Well, it serves me right!" bellowed the wolf, crawling back to the woods with his tail between his legs. "I am in the butcher business, not the medical business!"

STEP 1: REFLECT ON YOUR CHILDHOOD INTERESTS

"Step out of the history that is holding you back. Step into the new story you are willing to create." –Oprah Winfrey

When your 3rd grade teacher asked what you wanted to be when you grew up, you may have answered something like, "doctor," "firefighter," or even "Iron Man." Maybe as you grew up, your answer changed to "author," "police officer," or "rock star," and so on. Take a few minutes now and jot down what you instinctively loved to do as a kid. What brought you sheer joy? What did you do purely for fun? What activities were you engaged in when you realized you had lost all sense of time? Aspects from those things you naturally gravitated towards and were inherently good at can now translate into a fulfilling career for you.

Did you love to read in some quiet corner every day of the week? Were you a puzzle fanatic? Did you often find yourself being the first to volunteer for an unfamiliar or complex task? Could you wile away the hours coloring, drawing, or painting? Did you sing to yourself wherever you went? Were you the life of the party, always ready to do something wild for the sake of a laugh? Did you speak authoritatively as a 5-year-old, instructing everyone where to sit for Thanksgiving Dinner? Were you a natural ham, fearlessly addressing your family members or another group? Did you get competitive in sports? On the sports field, were you pointing out where everyone should stand and where the ball would be coming?

Granted, today you are not the same person you were as a child. So how does the advice in Step 1 help? Well, these innate tendencies are all extremely indicative of who you might still be now.

If you loved to color or found yourself singing all of the time, you might enjoy working as an art director or music teacher. If you had an interest in the medical field and authoring books, you might have a love for inventing new ways to solve complex problems. Perhaps your decision to defend the defenseless, despite the risk to your own safety, speaks of a deep-seated desire to build a non-profit that can reach those in need. Maybe you are a natural in the spotlight, and would enjoy life as an Influencer on Instagram.

The key is to find the common thread between each interest and the professional attribute from each inborn talent. Once you find a potential link, make a note for yourself as reference as you continue onward. As you write, the answers to some of these questions will start to unfold.

STEP 2: IDENTIFY WHAT DRAINS AND ENERGIZES YOU

"People inspire you, or they drain you. Pick them wisely." –Hans F. Hanson

Oftentimes, people find themselves on a career path that was once appealing but has since become the bane of their existence. Clocking in for the sake of anything more than receiving a paycheck at the end of the pay period can be laughable or even terribly painful. At one point, however, it was a delight to head to work in the morning. What gives?

Misplaced priorities and not really knowing who you are can create this vicious cycle when you are at the beginning of the application process. Ignoring that little voice inside you that said, "yuck," to that high-paying offer might come back to bite you. That is why it is very important to consider what could drain you over a long period of time.

If you find that interacting with 100 new faces every day leaves you feeling utterly exhausted by closing time, you should think twice about accepting customer service positions. When repetitive tasks in a quiet, fairly inactive environment leave you defeated by dinner, maybe you should not apply for an opening in the back office of an accounting firm.

On the reverse, maybe you tend to be highly organized, but the constant changes in demand within a restaurant environment excite you. Or, the fast pace of event planning is something you have expertly navigated before, but the cyclical nature of leading a meditation class is actually what motivates you.

Pinpointing where your energy source comes from can be challenging. Here is a quick tip: after practicing something for a day (i.e. going somewhere quiet and reading), do you feel relaxed or anxious? Try it out with different types of activities and see what happens. Record your thoughts.

STEP 3: WRITE OUT YOUR IDEAL LIFESTYLE

"If you don't design your own life plan, chances are you'll fall into someone else's plan. And, guess what they have planned for you? Not much." –Jim Rohn

Daydreaming is common for people with aspirations. Pondering life with a few differences here and there is the necessary seed from which your life-changing maneuvers stem from. For those less optimistic, you might be afraid to think past your very next step. However, to invoke a cliché, dare to dream.

Imagine where you would live. Would it be in a city apartment, overlooking downtown? Does homesteading in a rural community suit you? What sounds do you hear in this space? Are cows bleating or horns honking? Can you smell your neighbor's cooking or a wildflower scent wafting in from the field next to your dwelling? Would you like to look out over a significant amount of land space, or do buildings, lights, sidewalks and people always strolling by fuel you?

What would you like most: traveling internationally every month? Is it to become a known regular at your local breakfast diner, or a volunteer with environmentally focused non-profits?

Would you have a family of humans, animals, all or none of the above?

Might you prefer to rest regularly on weekends or live flexibly every week?

Long-term goals are the very stuff that motivates the world's most successful people. Without knowing yourself and having a fully formed objective, it is too easy to lose your way and end up feeling discouraged. Therefore, think of your goal(s) as your Northern Star, guiding you to where you want to go.

Get out your notebook and start freewriting, create a decorative poster full of representative icons, or design a colorful dream board full of vivid photos. Whatever method you choose, put together a real, hard-copy outline of what your life would look like if you had everything exactly as you would prefer. You will see your goals forming and solidifying before your eyes.

STEP 4: TAKE REPUTABLE PERSONALITY TESTS

"Personality is like a charioteer with two headstrong horses, each wanting to go in different directions." –Martin Luther King, Jr.

There are numerous personality tests to choose from. They range from determining what kind of car you like to what your color preferences mean for your future. When it comes to finding out what might lie deep in your subconscious, or what habits you may possess without even realizing it, personality and career assessments that use distinguished psychological techniques are your best friends. Many time-honored methods such as the Meyers-Briggs Type Indicator have supporting works that explain the tendencies of each Type (Introvert vs. Extrovert, etc.) when found in varying roles of life.

One free Meyers-Briggs style assessment is located here: http://www.humanmetrics.com/cgi-win/jtypes2.asp It is called the Jung Typology Test and is brought to you by HumanMetrics.com.

To get the best idea of who you might be according to these evaluations, always answer as truthfully as possible. There are no right or wrong answers. Every person is different, and every person has less-popular sides to their personalities. That means when you are asked, "Would you rather run screaming into the ocean than speak in front of a group of forty strangers?" it is okay to say, "Yes."

Once you receive the results, read the detailed explanation and decide what does and does not apply to you. If too many attributes sound off to you, give the questionnaire another try. Perhaps the test itself is not very thorough, in which case you might want to give other evaluations a chance.

However, keep in mind that every person is different. Even if your results are essentially the same across the board, allow some room for your uniqueness to fill in those areas that are not quite right.

The evaluation process alone can help you become more self-aware. Use the results as a tool for decoding how you interact with society and yourself.

CHAPTER 2:

Discover Perspective

"Whatever you do, do it well. Do it so well that when people see you do it they will want to come back and see you do it again and they will want to bring others and show them how well you do what you do." –Walt Disney

By the conclusion of the first chapter, you will have likely gained a detailed understanding of the person you are, internally. Yet, who are you from the outside looking in? The next four steps are sure to get you there.

STEP 5: SURVEY YOUR FRIENDS AND FAMILY

"Surround yourself with people who see your value and remind you of it." –livelifehappy.com

A person's memories of their own childhood are wholly dependent on what they were focused on in each instance. Like the time when you hailed the ice cream truck with your grandmother and all you remember is how delicious the chocolate-dipped cone tasted. What you do not recall from that moment was that you had earlier been upset because it was mid-summer and you were missing your school friends. Your grandmother knew that you needed a little pick-me-up and a tasty treat would be just the trick. Add to that, your grandmother was impressed by your fortitude and young leadership in getting that truck to stop for tiny 'ole you!

Similarly, people can often live their adult lives aware only of what they are focused on at any given time. Therefore, it is greatly beneficial to ask for some outside perspective, preferably from those who have your best interests in mind.

Whenever you find yourself at a gathering of friends or family, take some time to ask them what they believe are your interests and skills. Be sure to ask why they believe those things. Take a little notebook with you and jot down their comments so you can remind yourself later. Or, ask them to email you their thoughts so you have a record of them. It is too easy to forget if you just rely on your memory.

Becky Gosky

The unique perspective of a loved one can sometimes bring to light those hidden gifts you had been unaware of, previously. Perhaps your family would recall you always surrounded by younger cousins who were sitting in rapt attention. They might suggest a field involving children. Maybe you thought everyone believed you had a talent for opera singing, but Aunt Andrea gently delivered the difficult news that you, in fact, do not.

Take care not to be disheartened by unmet expectations, however. Tough love and bolstered presumptions alike can be powerful motivators.

STEP 6: ASK COWORKERS AND SUPERVISORS TO DESCRIBE YOU

"A truly great co-worker is hard to find, difficult to part with, and impossible to forget."
-Redbubble

In a work environment, people often behave differently than they would in more personal or casual settings. Sometimes a person takes on a more reserved, hyper-focused demeanor, or could appear to be more energetic and sociable than outside of work. While this may seem disingenuous, rather it should be viewed more like a separate collection of tendencies while acting within a different role.

As an employee, colleague, or supervisor, a person may have different skillsets that effect each role differently. Consider requesting someone from each of your roles to review your usual behaviors. You might ask your supervisor, someone who reports to you, an office peer, or a teacher or student of yours.

What do they have to say about what causes you stress? How do they believe you handle those situations? Are you an effective leader and a responsible teammate? Would they consider you charismatic or analytical? Do you like to participate in the office birthday celebrations? Are you known for organizing and sending get-well gift baskets to those who are out on medical leave?

That kind of perspective from those who are familiar with you on a professional level is invaluable for purposes on the career front. Effective feedback from a variety of colleagues adds another level of depth to the truths of who you are from the outside perspective.

STEP 7: DEFINE YOURSELF

"The more you think is possible, the more is actually possible." –Katrina Lake, Founder of Stitch Fix

It is too easy to be caught up in simply rolling with the punches and surviving the day. People can often behave a certain way in daily life without realizing their own habits. We might be in a rut for years without realizing it.

Stop and reflect. What does your typical work day look like? How do you consistently handle stressful situations? When do you become engaged and light up? What drains you? What invigorates you? What do you find yourself volunteering for without even having to think about it? When you put those behaviors together, what sort of person might you appear to be?

Do you come across as educated and well spoken? Do you maintain a reputation of being kind and reliable? Are you the quiet person who produces excellent content every time?

Spend a week's time being hyper-aware of your actions and write out your thoughts. How do you interact with people when you are relaxed or stressed? What time of day do you feel you are the most creative or the most fatigued? Where do you go when you need a break? If you take a walk at lunch, do you invite others to join you or need that alone time? While in the office, do you chat with everyone you see or do you generally keep to yourself? Once the week is up, go back and review what you noticed and determine the kind of person you feel you portray yourself as.

STEP 8: SEEK WISDOM

"The truest wisdom is a resolute determination." –Napoleon Bonaparte

Modern society delights in a spectacular era lovingly referred to as "the information age." What does this mean? It means experts in almost every field and the wisdom they offer are within reach more than ever before.

Think about who might know a thing or two about your ideal lifestyle. Who are the experts in your ideal field? Is it a small business owner? Is it an at-home parent? How about a savvy marketing genius or a skillful researcher? Find someone who has lived the lifestyle you aspire to and request some time to chat. Then, simply, ask away!

Some questions to ask:

Is your dream lifestyle possible? How did they start their own journey? What obstacles did they face? How did they overcome those obstacles? What is their typical day like? And so on.

Start first within your community. There is no substitute for a face-to-face meeting. You can read in their body language what energizes or depletes them just as clearly as the words they speak. Check to see if there are meet-ups for like-minded professionals, or service organizations attended by small business owners. Every community has civic organizations you can join. They are a great way to get to know and trust others who have been on this journey before you. Usually once they get to know you, they are more than willing to share. Do not be afraid to ask someone you especially admire to mentor you. You may be just the person they have been waiting to help!

A story to provide perspective:

From Aesop's, "The Lion, the Donkey, and the Fox."

Message: Learn from the Failures of Others.

The Story: A lion, donkey and fox all go out hunting together. How this came to be, I am not sure! Anyway, they were successful and at the end of the day, gathered around a huge amount of meat. Then came the task of dividing all the meat.

The lion, being the King of the Jungle, commanded that the donkey divide the meat. The donkey, being hopelessly gullible, split the meat into equal portions so they could all enjoy the feast.

The Lion was angered by this decision and with a swipe of his paw, killed the poor donkey.

The lion then required the fox to parcel out the meat. Being very sly, the fox immediately pushed the majority of the meat over to the lion, leaving a tiny portion for himself.

"Who taught you to divide so equitably?" asked the lion. The fox replied, "I learned it from the donkey."

The Lesson: Learn from the experience (and sometimes misfortunes) of others. Failing is only final if you give up.

If no one in your local community fits any of those descriptions you have listed, searching online is your next step. Perhaps there is a blog article or two offering insights from someone who, once upon a time, was just like you, starting out. Perhaps the website of a successful fashion designer has a section where questions are welcome.

Another great option is to read a book. For centuries, wisdom has been passed down generation to generation through this ancient method. As sure as humanity's existence, someone has likely been in your shoes, working toward a similar life.

Seek out an opinion or two from these reliable sources and add them to the figurative "kettle of considerations" that is undoubtedly percolating in your head by now.

CHAPTER 3:

Discover New Things

"The real voyage of discovery consists not in seeking new landscapes, but in having new eyes." –Marcel Proust

When is the last time you dared to explore a new activity or strange city? If you find that your life is painfully predictable, these next few steps might help shake things up and allow room for inspiration. Keep going...you are worth it!

STEP 9: SAMPLE NEW MEDIA

"Don't use social media to impress people; use it to impact people." – Dave Willis

Start with simple changes. If you enjoy political commentary, try listening to a different political podcast with similar views. Then, try inching your way across the aisle. Take the plunge at some point and dive into something completely different, like a story-telling or musically focused podcast.

Join a Facebook group made up of inventors or entrepreneurs. Follow an Instagram influencer who teaches about financial security. Get creative with accounts or pages you might find helpful or entertaining.

When folks listen to the same podcasts, watch the same vlog channels, and spend time on the same social media platforms chatting with the same people, they can unintentionally fall into this trap known as an "echo chamber." While there is no direct problem in engaging with like-minded individuals, it can indirectly create cyclical thinking, which in turn, can hinder personal growth. To combat that potential negative influence, reach beyond your usual comfort zone.

STEP 10: ENGAGE YOUR SENSES

"There are not seven wonders of the world in the eyes of a child. There are seven million." –Walt Streightiff

Imagine this:

You sink your teeth into a cushion of decadent chocolate and you are lifted into a dream of bitter hazelnut and sweet cream. You hear the lilting twitter of a songbird with feathers donning colors you have never seen before. The earthen scent of fresh lain soil lingering with fragrant swirls of stargazer lilies fills your nostrils, carried near by the gentle brush of a cool breeze. You soon find yourself enveloped by a state of heavenly bliss.

Humans are designed to process information through their senses. That may be obvious, but it is a fact people often forget to consider when seeking a change of lifestyle.

Taste new flavors. Smell different fragrances. Observe strange patterns. Hear unfamiliar tones. Feel bizarre textures. If you find yourself eating the same foods, experiencing the same environments, listening to the same music, you will likely not do anything differently from what you already have been.

Sometimes all it takes to find inspiration is engaging the primitive aspects of yourself.

STEP 11: GO SOMEWHERE NEW

"Blessed are the curious for they shall have adventures." —Lovelle Drachman

How about these places?

- ✓ In southeastern California, there is a farming community in the middle of the desert. Football is a necessity of life there and if you do not like enchiladas, it is only because you have yet to try them. Join a local church while visiting and you might as well have lived there your entire life.

- ✓ The panhandle of Florida is home to a town nestled amongst trees, broken down trucks, and brick-paved roads leading to colonial homes. There are hidden gems for photography made up of long abandoned factories and secret lake views. A sense of unlocked potential and creativity emanates from everywhere you turn.

- ✓ Deep in the north Midwestern U.S. is a land of harsh-weather-aficionados and driving well under the speed limit. The people of its communities hold fast to their protective instincts for their environment, standing firm in their roles as guardians of the nature, which surrounds them.

Diversity can be found as closely as the next town over. When you can experience a culture with a different history, inundated with different ideas, and faced with different challenges, you discover new ways to engage the world around you. Unable to travel long distances? Explore a new community park, a mom-and-pop lunch joint, or venture to the coffee shop on the other side of town.

STEP 12: TRY DIFFERENT INDUSTRIES

"Interesting people are interested people." –Becky Gosky, *Your GPS for Life*

A small manufacturing company temporarily hired you to take over bookkeeping while their permanent employee was out on maternity leave. Now she has returned and you are left job-hunting once again. You did not enjoy bookkeeping, but because you have the experience, you apply to every open bookkeeping position you can find.

It is true that you will be more likely to land a job in which you have the most experience, but if it is your dream career you are after, that is not the way to find it. Therefore, try a field of work you have not worked within before. Perhaps, instead of bookkeeping for manufacturing companies, you might like a sales position in real estate.

If you are not yet ready to stake your livelihood on such a gamble, try these options first as a new hobby, instead. Participate in a painting class over the weekend. Take a crash course in web design. Attend a trade school for electrical engineering. Shadow a plumber or a college professor.

Sample any industry that sparks your interest and maybe even a few that do not. You never know what might catch fire within you.

CHAPTER 4:

Discover Your Calling

"The two most important days in your life are the day you were born, and the day you find out why." –Mark Twain

Now that you know who you are, where your talents lie, and what inspires you, you are ready for the final stretch. These last five steps are vital to your journey of self-discovery. Onward!

STEP 13: FOLLOW YOUR INTUITION

"Know your WHY to know your WAY." —Becky Gosky, Your GPS for Life

Have you ever had a powerful draw toward a particular something you encountered, but you could not explain why? A feeling that you should not go down a certain street, only to later find out that a drunk driver had barreled down that road at exactly the moment you would have been there? On the other hand, you had a strong urge to choose what were eventually announced to be winning numbers on your lottery ticket. Your inner voice is speaking to you.

If you enjoy baking, but for reasons unknown, you feel pulled to go to nursing school, go the latter route. That sudden need to do one thing over another is what some call a "gut feeling," or intuition. It is a powerful knowing that we all possess but do not always obey. However, when it comes to making decisions that will alter the trajectory of your life, there is no greater ally.

STEP 14: MAKE YOUR CASE

"Your life changes the moment you make a new, congruent, and committed decision." –Tony Robbins

Case Study #1:

You are someone who loves to create new and exciting designs. You are in tune with trends and find the race to stay ahead exhilarating. You are personable, knowledgeable, and you have the means to get started. You simply know you were meant to pursue a career as a marketing brand designer.

Case Study #2:

You are calculating and disciplined, with a well-honed talent to strategize. What's more, you find it deeply satisfying when you help others make sense of their own finances. It is high time you decided to start an investments advising firm.

Collect all of your discoveries over the course of this guide and begin to piece them together like a big "you" puzzle. Lay out the evidence of why you feel you should pursue one career over another. Complete the process with making a decision based on that gut feeling you have and you are ready to take the next step.

STEP 15: SAY "NO" TO LOW PRIORITIES

"You will say no to a lot of good things to say yes to a lot of great things."
–Becky Gosky, Your GPS for Life

One thing that every successful businessperson will tell you is that they say "no" often. The misconception is that in order to really get somewhere in a career or when starting a new business, you need to be extremely agreeable and seize every opportunity to network or get the word out about your talents.

The truth of the matter is that every time you say "yes" to something, you are saying "no" to something else.

If you say you will attend a local college football game with some acquaintances, you are declining the opportunity to speak with some potential investors who planned a meeting at that same time. When you schedule time to make sales calls for your business, you are choosing not to participate in the foosball tournament taking place that day.

Again, there are no right or wrong answers. Balance what keeps you moving forward professionally with what replenishes your energy. Prioritizing your passions over less important things is an absolute necessity if you want to be successful.

STEP 16: CLING TO WHAT MOTIVATES YOU

"Whatever you vividly imagine, ardently desire, sincerely believe, and enthusiastically act upon, must inevitably come to pass." –Paul J. Meyer

Sometimes such a drastic life change can be overwhelming and it can be all too easy to lose sight of what brought you to this point. Walk yourself back through these steps and remind yourself why you are taking them. Make additional note of those things that stand out and spur you forward.

Furthermore, take a break on occasion! Everyone needs those moments to refresh and refocus. Stop working and do something completely different for a little while. Go on a walk, shut off the screens, get a massage, read a book, talk with a close friend, engage in something that allows your mind and body to rest. When you feel ready to get back to work, review these steps to discovery and remember to enjoy what you are doing.

CONCLUSION

Never Give Up!

"Today I will do what others won't so tomorrow I can do what others can't." –Becky Gosky, *Your GPS for Life*

A story to provide perspective:

From Aesop's, "The Tortoise and the Hare."

Message: Never Give Up.

The Story: A rabbit (hare) is speedy, as we all know. Unfortunately, he is boastful about it, too. He challenges all of the other animals to a foot race to see who can beat him. He knows he is the best and trusts that no one can. He taunts them all with his most obnoxious bravado.

One of his friends, the turtle (tortoise) accepts his challenge. He thinks, "well……why…not?"

The rabbit thinks it is a funny joke and gibes the turtle. "You cannot outrun me, Turtle! How hilarious of you to even think so," he laughs. Nevertheless, the turtle is serious.

Soon after, the race begins. The rabbit starts out at a feverish pace, gesticulating with glee about how much in the lead he is. To further mock the turtle, the rabbit decides to take a nap exclaiming,

"You are so plodding, Turtle! I can sleep for hours and still you cannot beat me!"

The turtle simply keeps going and going along his steady pace, never giving up the race.

By the time the rabbit wakes up, he turns and sees the turtle about to cross the finish line! He panics and starts for the finish line, too. But, the turtle was simply too far ahead of him and wins the race right out from under him.

The Lesson: Slow and steady wins the race. At times, you will notice others around you who seem to have all the answers and a big head start. However, everyone faces obstacles. It is those of us to keep going every day despite the obstacles that win the race.

Congratulations! You have completed the steps to discovering your career passion. Break out the champagne, toss those streamers, and celebrate yourself. Be proud that you have decided to make a change in your life that will make every day a little sweeter.

The road ahead will not be devoid of its struggles, but do not fear. With your newfound confidence in yourself and your goals in sight, remember that living your ideal lifestyle is well within your grasp. Follow your gut, cling to what is important, and dive right in!

Never give up. You've got this.

AUTHOR'S NOTE

If you liked, "*Land That Job! 16 Simple Steps to Discover Your Career Passion,*" please consider reading my other books in the *Land That Job!* Series on Amazon.

Please leave me a review while you are there. Your comments truly shape the future of my work. Thank you!

For more hands-on help, I offer certified coaching through the Your GPS for Life Community. Check us out at **www.yourgpsforlife**, on Facebook: @yourgpsforlife, and on LinkedIn: linkedin.com/company/yourgps.

You will receive a complimentary thank you gift for contacting us and subscribing!

www.ingramcontent.com/pod-product-compliance
Lightning Source LLC
Chambersburg PA
CBHW070843220526
45466CB00002B/870